Horse Racing 101

150 trivia Questions and Answers

3R Series – Review, Recognize and Remember

James Magee

Published by Novel Characters, 444 North Paula Drive, Suite 334, Dunedin, FL 34698

First paperback printing was in 2011.

The aim of this book . . .

Horseracing 101 will be the tenth book in a series of books subtitled Review-Remember-Recognize. The first book is titled American History. The second book was titled World History. The third and fourth books were respectively titled The Constitution of the United State and Classic Novels (Authors and their Titles) . The sixth and seventh books were respectively titled Who Wrote this Book? and Art History Review. The eighth and ninth books are Music History Review and Rock 'n Roll Review. The 150 questions and answers in this book discuss the basics of horse racing.

This book examines what a novice needs to know to understand this sport - with special emphasis on the Triple Crown of Thoroughbred Horse Racing in the U.S. The information and facts discussed is taken directly from research found on the Internet (wikipedia.com). It falls under the umbrella of public domain. Since each question is randomly chosen, the book can be opened to any page at any time.

"Horse sense is the thing a horse has which keeps it from betting on people."

W. C. Fields

"A true gambler never gambles – he always has a sure thing."

Unknown

QUESTION # 1

What is the Morning Line in horse racing and how can it benefit someone who wants to bet on a horse race?

QUESTION # 2

While Win, Place and Show represent separate bets on the 1st three horses in a race (the 1st horse pays a win bet – the 2nd horse pays a place bet – and the 3rd horse pays for show), what does it mean to bet an Exacta, a Quinella and a Trifecta which are known as "gimmick bets"?

ANSWER # 1

Morning Lines are computed by an official track handicapper. The line doesn't reflect how actual betting will proceed – it just provides a framework for bettors to use in calculating ("doping out") which horses they want to bet on. Basically, it acts as a guide for assessing which horses are better.

ANSWER # 2

An Exacta bettor bets two separate horses to win and place that will only pay in that order. In a Quinella, one bets two horses to win and place – their order of finish makes no difference. A Trifecta bettor bets three horses to win, place and show in a specific order that will only pay in that specific order.

QUESTION # 3

What other bets – beside Win, Place, Show, an Exacta, a Quinella, and a Trifecta - can a bettor make?

QUESTION # 4

What are bettors referring to when they say things like "I am betting the chalk." or it is a "chalk horse" or "It is a chalk race"?

ANSWER # 3

Other bets are the Daily Double where one plays the first horse (Win) in the 1st race and the 1st horse (Win) in the 2nd race – bets are made before the 1st race. The Trifecta Box is made where you play all the combinations of three horses in all different orders. This can be either a $1 or $2 dollar bet.

ANSWER # 4

"Chalk" in horse racing parlance refers to a horses that are considered favorites or have the most money bet on them. This pre-computer term goes back to when "bookies" wrote bets on blackboards. The names of favorites would disappear in chalk dust as their odds were constantly being lowered.

QUESTION # 5

The U.S. Triple Crown consists of three races: The Kentucky Derby (Churchill Downs), The Preakness Stakes (Pimlico Race Course) and The Belmont Stakes (Belmont Race Course). Which is the longest and shortest race out of these three?

QUESTION # 6

While all bets can be made at the track with the aid of computers (they generate betting tickets) that are provided for the public away from the betting windows, only certain bets can be made only on the computer. What are they?

ANSWER # 5

The Preakness Stakes (Pimlico Racecourse) is the shortest dirt track race of the U.S. Triple Crown (1 and 3/16th of a mile). The Kentucky Derby (Churchill Downs) is 1and ¼ of a mile on dirt while the Belmont Stakes (Belmont Racecourse) is the longest dirt track of the three at a mile and a half.

ANSWER # 6

One computerized bet is the Superfecta which can be a Pick 4 (4 Win horses in 4 races that are designated by the track officials). These races can even be played for as little as .10 cents a bet or whatever they want. Bettors can also bet the Pick 6 which may run from the 6th to the 11th races (Wins).

QUESTION # 7

What are the two major areas where spectators may go to view the races after they enter the race track?

QUESTION # 8

Where else can bettors get this same information in order to make the best bet?

ANSWER # 7

Upon entering the track, a bettor has a choice between the Grandstands or the Club House. The distinction between the two is money. There is no charge for the Grandstand – but one must pay a fee for choosing the Club House. Providing a better view and better facilities for food sets them apart.

ANSWER # 8

The information that can be viewed on the tote board is also piped into hundreds of monitors, TV screens and online services. Bettors at the track are always exposed to this information as they move around the interior of the track area. There also are a number of separate odds boards for each race.

QUESTION # 9

What are the different kinds of races that a bettor may bet on depending on the type of track the bettor attends?

QUESTION # 10

What is the origin of the term "Triple Crown of Thoroughbred Racing" (shortened to U.S. Triple Crown) and who was responsible for inventing this term?

ANSWER # 9

Horse racing includes flats (on dirt), trotters and steeplechases. The flats have horses on dirt or synthetic surface. The steeplechases involve "jumps" and may be on turf. Finally, the trots have horses that pull a sulky and driver. All these races can be run on the same or different tracks based on surfaces.

ANSWER # 10

An unsettled controversy exists to this day over when and how this term originated. While some attribute it to Racing Form sports writer, Charles Hatton, after Gallant Fox won the title (1930 - eleven years after Sir Barton won it), the New York Times claimed that it had used this term in 1923.

QUESTION # 11

What is the sulky that is used in harness racing involving trotter horses (horses that maintain a gait known as a trot – it is important to winning that this trot is maintain throughout the entire race)?

QUESTION # 12

Why is the Morning Line – the earliest posted odds for each horse racing at the beginning of the day - constructed in such a way that they give the horses approximately 120% odds instead of 100 % odds?

ANSWER # 11

A sulky is a light two-wheeled horse-drawn vehicle driven by a driver, used chiefly in harness racing. Much of harness racing is run at night.

ANSWER # 12

Like any other business such as a bank, the track exists to make money. The reason why the Morning Line is constructed giving the horses roughly 120% odds is because of the track's commission fees that are included. The track must generate revenue – and this is where they begin.

QUESTION # 13

What is the difference between trotting and pacing when one is discussing harness racing?

QUESTION # 14

What is a "Program," where can a bettor obtain one, how much does it cost and how is it different from the information a bettor receive from the Daily Racing Form or the tote board?

ANSWER # 13

Trotting and pacing in harness racing refer to the type of gait (stride) that is set at the start by the pacer or trotter horse (a guide) and maintain throughout the race. Pacers usually run with a different stride than trots. If a driver breaks the stride they must fall back and regain the stride before competing again.

ANSWER # 14

Programs are bought at the track's entrance for about $1.50. Programs list the day's races along with post positions, jockey colors, the morning line, the jockey, the owner, the trainer, the stable or farm the horse came from, etc. The Daily Racing Form lists all the tracks and a horse's past performances.

QUESTION # 15

How many winners has there been of the U.S. Triple Crown? How many can you name? Do you know the years that they won this historic U. S. racing event?

QUESTION # 16

Where can a bettor buy the Daily Racing Form (from here on this tabloid newspaper will be referred to as the DRF), how much does it cost and how will it benefit the bettor's chances of winning?

ANSWER # 15

As follows, there have been 11 winners of the Triple Crown: Sir Barton (1919), Gallant Fox (1930), Omaha (1935), War Admiral (1937), Whirlaway (1941), Count Fleet (1943), Assault (1946), Citation (1948), Secretariat (1973), Seattle Slew (1977), and Affirmed (1978).

ANSWER # 16

Besides buying the DPF at the track, a bettor can buy this tabloid newspaper before at many newspaper stands and kiosks for about $7.00. The DRF offers the edge to the bettor by providing the horse's past performances along with exclusive handicapping and wagering tools.

QUESTION # 17

What is the Morning Telegraph and what was its relationship to the DRF?

QUESTION # 18

What became of both of these thoroughbred racing papers over time?

ANSWER # 17

The DRF was founded in Chicago, IL in 1894. It was America's racing tabloid newspaper in the West and Midwest while the Morning Telegraph (with its broadsheet format) shared the market with the DRF in the East. Their staffs even had separate press rooms in the same building.

ANSWER # 18

Both of these Annenberg publications that shared common business, statistical and editorial staffs over time realized their separate destinies. The Morning Telegraph disappeared in 1972 because of unions while the DRF was eventually sold to Arlington Capital Partners in Washington, D.C.

QUESTION # 19

How did the Daily Racing Form survive the strikes by the New York Typographical Union (printer's union) and continue printing their paper in the broadsheet mode that was popular due to the now defunct Morning Telegraph?

QUESTION # 20

Are the scheduled races for each of the three jewels of the U.S. Triple Crown the same for each year?

ANSWER # 19

The way the DRF survived was that they moved most of their equipment to Hightstown, New Jersey just outside the jurisdiction of the ITU and began using what is known as "cold print." Eventually, in 1972 they took over for the Morning Telegraph and printed the Eastern edition of the DRF.

ANSWER # 20

Yes, the Kentucky Derby (described as "The Most Exciting Two Minutes in Sports") occurs on the 1st Saturday in May; the Preakness Stakes follows two weeks later on the 3rd week in May; and the Belmont Stakes falls on the 1st Saturday in June – 5 weeks after the Derby.

QUESTION # 21

What information is available to the bettor on the "Tote Board" which is the large numeric or alphanumeric display which is located in the track's infield?

QUESTION # 22

What track conditions are very important to the bettor at a dirt track and where can the bettor obtain this information?

ANSWER # 21

The "Tote Board" gives the time of day, the post time to the next race, approximate odds for each horse in the last race, the results and the payoffs of the last race, approximate odds of each horse in the next race, the track conditions, equipment and jockey changes, and potential payments for some exotic bets.

ANSWER # 22

The bettor should know whether a dirt track is Fast, Slow, Muddy, Good or Sloppy. Some horses are "mudders" – they run well in the mud while others don't. The bettor will get this information from the tote board located on the infield of the track itself.

QUESTION # 23

What does it mean when a bettor gives the cashier at the window $6.00 and tells the cashier that the bet is on a particular horse like the 2 or the 7 and that the bettor wants to bet that horse "across the board?"

QUESTION # 24

After a bettor arrives at a dirt track in time to prepare for the start of the 1st race and the Daily Double, buys a program (and a Daily Racing Form) and examines the morning line on the odds board, the info on the Tote Board, what should the bettor do next in order to place an informed, calculated bet?

ANSWER # 23

"Across the board" means that the bettor wants to bet the horse identified by its number for Win, Place and Show - $2.00 to Win, $2.00 to Place and $2.00 to show. If the horse wins, the bettor also gets Place and Show money – the same situation exists if the horse places – place and show money.

ANSWER # 24

Before going to see the Paddock parade, one should find a quiet area and handicap ("dope out") the next race. Has your horse won any races recently? Has your horse won on this course and at this distance before? How did your horse fare on this type of surface before? What is your horse's weight?

QUESTION # 25

While Diane Crump was the first female rider to be registered in a thoroughbred race at Hialeah Park Race Course (1969), which woman jockey was the only female to win a part of the U.S. Triple Crown?

QUESTION # 26

How can a bettor resolve the problem of making a realistic bet while the odds keep changing from the morning line once the betting starts?

ANSWER # 25

Retired American jockey, Julie Krone, was the first female jockey to win part of the U.S. Triple Crown when she won the Belmont Stakes in 1993 aboard Colonial Affair. She is also the first woman jockey to reach the Racing Hall of Fame and win the Breeders' Cup race when she rode Halfbridled.

ANSWER # 26

A bettor resolves the problem of changing odds by holding off their wager and waiting for the most opportune moment to place a bet. The downside to waiting too long is that the window may close by the time they get to it if there is any delay on the line – thereby, preventing them from placing their bet.

QUESTION # 27

What is the significance of the poles to jockeys that surround the track in full view of the jockeys as they ride their mounts?

QUESTION # 28

Why is important to the bettor to know about the term, furlong (from furrow length)?

ANSWER # 27

Most horses would probably die if they raced around the track at break neck speed. They must be restrained and run the track at moderated speeds. This is the sole responsibility of the jockey that is mounted. The poles are distance poles – they are spaced in a deliberate fashion for the jockeys.

ANSWER # 28

Furlongs are used in horse racing as a measure of length when discussing a horse race. There are 8 furlongs in a mile, so 1/8 of a mile equals one furlong. An average horse race is about 6 furlongs in length. How a horse runs at different lengths is critical when a bettor is handicapping a race.

QUESTION # 29

How does a horse bettor learn about odds so they can make a sensible bet?

QUESTION # 30

Does a similar race to the U.S. Triple Crown exist for fillies?

ANSWER # 29

When a horse bettor puts up $2.00 for a win bet on a horse going off at 2 to 1 odds, the horse bettor will be paid $6.00 ($4.00 + the original $2.00 bet) in winnings. The horse bettor receives $2.00 for each dollar they put up. The higher the odds (10 to 1) are - the greater the risk and the gain.

ANSWER # 30

The Triple Tiara (formerly the Filly Triple Crown) exists for fillies on dirt tracks: the Kentucky Oaks at Churchill Downs (11/8 miles); the Black-Eyed Susan Stakes at Pimlico Race Course (1 1/8 miles); and the Acorn Stakes at Belmont Park (1 mile). The races differed from 2003 to 2007.

QUESTION # 31

How does the new or regular bettor benefit from watching the horses as they move around the Paddock or during the post parade when they move toward the starting gate?

QUESTION # 32

What are the three most important considerations when a bettor determines the payoff from different odds?

ANSWER # 31

Observing the horses during these two times allows the bettor to view the horse's body language and behavior – specifically the ears and tail. Horse's ear should work together and the tail should not be swishing. The horse should be "quiet," which means it should be gentle and controllable.

ANSWER # 32

The amount of money in that pool, the type of bet and the number of horses in that particular race are the most important consideration for determining a pay off. ($2 to win: "3 – 1" bet may pay $3 + $3 + $[1 – 2] = $7 & change. $2 to win: "5 – 1" may pay $5 + $5 + $[1 – 2] = $11 & change, etc).

QUESTION # 33

How is a birthday determined for "firstlings" [first new born(s)] or other new foals and how does this affect their competition status?

QUESTION # 34

What titles are assigned to the track officials responsible for the legal running of a horse race and what are their specific responsibilities before the race begins, during the race and after the race ends?

ANSWER # 33

A horse born has its birthday the New Years Day. A horse born in November of the year is a 2-year old on the next January 1st. If that same horse races against a horse born the following February after its November birth, it will be running against a 1-year old, even though they are only 3 months apart.

ANSWER # 34

A tattoo inside the horse's mouth must be verified in the Paddock area by the official known as an Identifier. His book confirmation prevents fraud by substitution. Then the horse and jockey are weighed by the Clerk of the Scales to verify that and earlier weighing that morning is a match.

QUESTION # 35

How many fillies have won the Triple Tiara?

QUESTION # 36

Who are the other officials who must perform certain tasks either at the beginning, during or at the end of any given race?

ANSWER # 35

There are 8 fillies that have won the Triple
Tiara: Dark Mirage (1968), Shuvee (1969),
Chris Evert (1974), Ruffian (1975), Davona
Dale (1979), Mom's Command (1985), Open
Mind (1989) and Sky Beauty (1993). No filly
won the reconfigured Triple Tiara during
2003-2006.

ANSWER # 36

Prior to Post Time (race begins), 8 or 9 gate
crew (non-officials) help the horses into their
chosen stalls. Once inside and ready, the
Started presses a button and they are off.
Some horses have to blind folded without the
rider to enter them. Horses have 3 chances
to break ("go!") before a track ban exists.

QUESTION # 37

Before Grey Lag won the Belmont Stakes (1921) [which was the 1st time the classic was run counter-clockwise, contrary to English rules], what kind of races were run according to the rules of the King's Plate which was set by Charles II in English racing?

QUESTION # 38

Who are the Stewards and why are their judgment calls about how a race was conducted more serious than a jockey's objection about a fellow jockey's actions?

ANSWER # 37

The King's Plate require two "heat" to win for 4 miles at a weight of 168 lbs. aboard a six year old horse. Eventually, these heats evolved into short "dashes" in American racing. These "dashes" evolved into the type of races we see today with three year olds and weights set by the Racing Secretary.

ANSWER # 38

Stewards are needed to oversee the race and make sure that everything is above board. After the race, they watch films of the race. A steward's inquiry (seen on the Tote Board) means a serious infraction has been lodged. This may result in disqualification of a horse and a fine on the jockey.

QUESTION # 39

One of the important criteria for calculating the best bet while handicapping is checking a horse's bloodline. What does the bettor have to look for to trace a horse's bloodline?

QUESTION # 40

When the Triple Tiara was reconfigured from 2003-2006, what races were run and where?

ANSWER # 39

Tracing bloodlines (checking a horse's heritage through its family tree – sired by which horse and dam) is as follows: Years ago, Ferdinand was listed in the Program and Daily Racing Form. Ferdinand descended from Nijinsky who descended from the famous horse named Northern Dancer.

ANSWER # 40

The reconfigured Triple Tiara consisted of the following races: the Mother Goose Stakes at Churchill Downs, the Coaching Club American Oaks at Pimlico Race Course and the Alabama Stakes, a 1 1/4 mile race run in August at Saratoga Race Course in Saratoga Springs, New York.

QUESTION # 41

What is the name of the horse that had a photo finish win during the 2010 Breeders' Cup Classic - finally beating the popular filly, Zenyatta, as she pursued her 20th consecutive straight win after winning 19 in a row?

QUESTION # 42

Is there a limit on how many races can be run on a race day and what is the time frame between the end of one race and the Post time of the next race?

ANSWER # 41

Blame (ridden by Garrett Gomez) beat
Zenyatta (ridden by Hall of Famer Mike
Smith) in the 2010 Breeders' Cup Classic
(Louisville, KY) in a photo finish. The
retired American superstar, filly Zenyatta was
owned by Jerry and Ann Moses. Zenyatta
failed to close as she moved from last place.

ANSWER # 42

The number of races run at any given track is
determined by the track. There is usually
anywhere between 9-13 races with Daily
Doubles possible at both ends. Most tracks
have a 25 minute period between races and
have the next race horses saddling up as the
horses that already ran are leaving the field.

QUESTION # 43

What famous annual horse race was nicknamed the "Street Car Derby" and why?

QUESTION # 44

What equipment does a jockey wear to insure a safe and successful ride?

ANSWER # 43

The Kentucky Derby during World War II was referred to as the "Street Car Derby" because of all the travel restriction imposed upon the American citizens during this crucial time. There were 65,000 attendees to see Count Fleet (1943) win even thought out-of-town tickets were not sold.

ANSWER # 44

To insure a safe and successful ride, a jockey wears or carries the following equipment: goggles (up to 7 pairs on a muddy surface – jockey peels them off as they fill up with mud), helmet and vest (protection during fall), whip, etc.

QUESTION # 45

Did any filly win the $2 million dollar bonus offered the reconfigured Triple Tiara during 2003-2006?

QUESTION # 46

How are bettors supposed to interpret the results of a race when they are told that a horse has won a race by a number of lengths?

ANSWER # 45

No filly won the $2 million dollar bonus offered in the reconfigured Triple Tiara during 2003-2006. The bonus had been offered by the New York Racing Association which was the operator of Belmont Park and Saratoga Race Track at the time. The bonus was discontinued in 2005.

ANSWER # 46

The rule of thumb in interpreting what is meant by a length is fairly simple. A length has been determined to be a fifth of a second. A horse that wins by 3 lengths has beaten the other horse by 1.5 seconds (3 x .5 = 1.5 secs).

QUESTION # 47

What are imposts as they relate to Handicap races?

QUESTION # 48

While the owner is responsible for the shoeing of his horses, hiring a vet, and paying shipping charges, what knowledge is required of a trainer beside the transportation of the owner's horses that will help him/her to pass the licensing exams that are necessary in the 50 states?

ANSWER # 47

In Handicap races, each horse must carry a specified weight called an impost which may be assigned by the Racing Secretary. Other factors like past performance and distance of the race may come under consideration – the end goal is to equalize the chances of the competitors.

ANSWER # 48

Future licensed trainers should know how to read a condition book, figure weight allowances, pick the best race for a horse to run in, the proper use of equipment, shoeing, bandaging, tying tongues, saddling for a race, bit burrs, and many other valuable training tips.

QUESTION # 49

What legal requirement must every track adhere to regarding an ambulance and a state certified veterinarian?

QUESTION # 50

While the Kentucky Derby ends with the winning horse wearing a traditional blanket of 554 red roses and the Belmont Stakes ends with the winner wearing a blanket of white carnations (New York), how does the Preakness Stakes handle the fact that black-eyed susans don't bloom until June?

ANSWER # 49

State law requires that an ambulance be present and follow each race run from behind. The law also requires that a state licensed Veterinarian be present at the track to help injured horses and if needed – perform humanly euthanizing procedures.

ANSWER # 50

Pimlico Race Track still gives a blanket of black-eyed susans to the winning horse. It substitutes Viking daisies for the black-eyed susans and then paints them to look like the flower that will bloom in June even though the Preakness is always run in the month of May.

QUESTION # 51

What are the different types of horses that you will be considering in horse race betting?

QUESTION # 52

Besides knowing how horses are classified by their age and sex, what other differences should be considered in making a bet regarding the competition?

ANSWER # 51

First born horses from a foal are called "firstlings" while other new born horses are yearlings. Horses are called geldings, fillies or colts until they are 5 years old – then they are called geldings (the same), mares or horses. Geldings are horses that have been neutered.

ANSWER # 52

The race being bet may be made up of many thoroughbreds while the horse being bet on might be a filly and not able to compete with stronger horses because of the length of the race. Usually, horses compete against their own sex and only have weight differences - focus should be on past performance.

QUESTION # 53

What is the Breeders' Cup, when and where is it held, and how did it originate?

QUESTION # 54

Aside from the fact that the Breeders' Cup has not always been run in the U.S. with U.S. horses, how many races does it actually run and how many horses are in each race on any given day?

ANSWER # 53

The Breeders' Cup is a two day event in which a series of thoroughbred horses race (mostly Grade 1) in different locations of the U.S. at the end of each horse racing year. This event was begun in 1982 by pet food heir, John R. Gaines in order to clean up the sport's image.

ANSWER # 54

The Breeders' Cup was run in Woodbine Race Track (Ontario, Canada – 1996) and allows entries from all over the world. A maximum of 14 starters are allowed in all 14 Breeders' Cup Championship races. The selection process includes qualifying races, a point system and "the Panel."

QUESTION # 55

While the traditional song sung at the Kentucky Derby is "My Old Kentucky Home" and the traditional song sung at the Preakness Stakes is "Maryland, My Maryland", what are the three songs that have been sung before the running of the Belmont Stakes at Belmont Race Track in New York?

QUESTION # 56

What other special event races occur during the Breeders' Cup and how is the attendance and how much money does the overall event accrue over its two day running?

ANSWER # 55

Prior to 1997, the song played at the Belmont Stakes was "Sidewalks of New York." From 1997 to 2009, "New York, New York" was played with Frank Sinatra as the vocalists as the jockeys headed to the starting gate. From 2010 on the song played has been "Empire State of Mind."

ANSWER # 56

Other special races run in the Breeders' Cup are: the Dirt Mile, Juvenile Fillies Turf, Filly and Mare Sprint, Juvenile Turf, Turf Sprint and Marathon. Attendance at the Breeders' Cup trails the Kentucky Derby, the Preakness Stakes and the Kentucky Oaks. In 2008, the gate was 25.5 million for 2 days.

QUESTION # 57

While California started giving bonuses beyond the purse and the Kentucky Derby added the 5th place winner in the purse (2005), the most popular payout is the format designed by Florida in 1975. Even though it has not been adopted by all the states, what is its breakdown?

QUESTION # 58

How did the term "bug boy" – which is the nickname given to any rookie or apprentice jockey – around the track amongst the racetrack personnel?

ANSWER # 57

In 1975, Florida tried to solve the problem of scratches and small fields by proposing this formula: 60% to the winning horse (owner pays the jockey and trainer) with 2nd through 4th becoming variable depending upon the size of the field. This was popular since a $60,000 yields $600 just for running.

ANSWER # 58

The term "bug boy," which has nothing to do with insects, was first used in reference to sports writers for the Daily Racing Form. It refers to the asterisk(s) that were put next to an apprentice (rookie) name indicating their weight allowance, their lack of experience or their lack of winners.

QUESTION # 59

While jockeys must know how to ride a horse, understand horse behavior and have riding experience, there are some definite levels (steps) of training that a future jockey must take to advance from apprentice jockey (bug boy) to journeyman. What are these steps (levels) that must be taken?

QUESTION # 60

Of the 3 jewels in the U.S. Triple Crown, which is the earliest race to be run and when did the other races appear on the scene?

ANSWER # 59

States differ. For most, minimum age is 16.
Usual weight is about 120 lbs (maintainable).
One must be physically fit (annual exams).
After running a number of races (varies), bug
boys use up their weight handicap allowance
along with their status and are either accepted
or denied "jockey" status and are licensed.

ANSWER # 60

The first race run of the three is now the
longest – the Belmont Stakes, which first ran
in 1867. This race was then followed by the
Preakness Stakes in 1873 – six years later.
The last race to appear was the Kentucky
Derby – first run in 1875. They appeared in
the reverse of their present order of running.

QUESTION # 61

Why is it illegal for anyone to give a horse something as harmless as a "milkshake"?

QUESTION # 62

What are standardbred horses?

ANSWER # 61

When the term "Milkshake" is used in horse racing, it does not refer to the type of drink one would buy at a soda fountain. A milkshake in this instance refers to pumping bicarbonate of soda through the horse's nose into its stomach lining. This prevents fatigue and masks the presence of other drugs.

ANSWER # 62

Compared to thoroughbred horses that run at a gallop with a saddle on, standardbred horses only run in harness at a trot or a pace.

QUESTION # 63

Where was the first million dollar horse race ever run in the U.S.?

QUESTION # 64

How many Kentucky Derby winners have sired other Kentucky Derby winners and who awards the garland and trophy?

ANSWER # 63

The first million dollar horse race run in the U.S. was run at Arlington Park in Chicago, IL. Appropriately, it was named the Arlington Million.

ANSWER # 64

There have been 12 winners of the Kentucky Derby who have sired future winners of the Kentucky Derby. One winner, Bold Venture, sired two future winners: Assault and Middleground. The garland and trophy are traditionally awarded by the Governor of Kentucky.

QUESTION # 65

Which jockey has won more than one U.S. Triple Crown? Was it Willie Shoemaker, Eddie Arcaro or Johnny Longdon?

QUESTION # 66

What are some of the obvious differences between English track racing and American track racing?

ANSWER # 65

The only jockey to win more than one U.S. Triple Crown was Eddie Arcaro (nicknamed "The Master"), who won two. He won when he was aboard Whirlaway in 1941 and aboard Citation in 1948. Johnny Longdon won the U.S. Triple Crown in 1943 aboard Count Fleet.

ANSWER # 66

England uses the combined form of the word horseracing while the U.S. splits the word into horse racing. While the U.S. names their races Race 1, Race 2, etc., the English name their races after times (the 1:40, the 3:10, etc.) or owner or trainers. The Americans run in the opposite direction (counter-clockwise).

QUESTION # 67

As of 2012, what major change will be enacted by pressure from the European Union upon England regarding the running of famous race, the John Smith Grand National, and other races like it in the future?

QUESTION # 68

While no U.S. President had ever attended the Kentucky Derby before 1968, a "first" occurred with regard to the Derby while a Presidential candidate was in attendance for the first time?

ANSWER # 67

As of 2012, England will be changing the direction that its horses run to anti-clockwise (like the U.S.) because of pressure from the European Union. The Chair and The Becher's Brook (fences) will undergo re-construction since the discovery that right turns are more auspicious for horseracing.

ANSWER # 68

Presidential candidate Richard Nixon had the distinction of viewing the first disqualification of a Kentucky Derby winner when the purse was taken away from first place winner, Dancer's Image, and given to the second place winner, Forward Pass, after testing positive for drugs during a urine test.

QUESTION # 69

After the race is over, how many horses are tested for drugs? Is it just the winning jockey and horse or the first three jockeys and their horses?

QUESTION # 70

Triple Crown winner Man O' War won 21 out of the 22 races that he ran. What was the ominous name of the horse that upset him?

ANSWER # 69

Actually, the first four horses and jockeys in every race have to be tested because of the bets being made (Pick 4). The first four winning horses are tested in the "spit-box" (in track parlance where the horse is administered a urine test and other drug tests.

ANSWER # 70

Man o' War (owned and bred by August Belmont, Jr.) was beaten by Upset. When August Belmont, Jr. joined the U.S. Army at 65 to serve during WWI, his wife named the new foal after her husband's exploits. Man o' War lost the race at Saratoga, known as the "Graveyard of Favorites".

QUESTION # 71

What are the six different colors of the horses who have won the Kentucky Derby and what is the breakdown of the colors in terms of wins?

QUESTION # 72

With regard to the Preakness Stakes, what jockey(s) holds the record for most consecutive wins?

ANSWER # 71

The six colors are Bay, Chestnut, Brown, Gray, Black and Roan. Winning Colors was the only roan horse to win it. The breakdown of the rest is as follows: 4 Black, 6 Gray, 17 Brown, 39 Chestnut and 60 Bay.

ANSWER # 72

The jockey, Pat Day, holds the record for the most consecutive wins with regard to the Preakness Stakes with 5; he is followed by Eddie Arcaro with 3 out of 4 consecutive and jockey, Bill Hartack, with 3 spread over a number of races.

QUESTION # 73

With regard to the Belmont Stakes, what trainer(s) holds the record for most consecutive wins?

QUESTION # 74

What does a jockey's agent do and how many apprentices and journeymen are a jockey Agent allowed to represent at any given time?

ANSWER # 73

The trainer Woody Stephens holds the record of consecutive wins in the Belmont Stakes with 5 between the years 1882-1887. He is followed by D. Wayne Lucas who had 3 consecutive wins between the years 1994-1996. Lucien Lauren follows these two with 2 consecutive wins between years 1972-1973.

ANSWER # 74

A jockey's agent is only allowed to represent one apprentice (known as a "bug boy" and two journeymen at any given time. At present, the retired Hall of Fame jockey, Angel Cordero, Jr. is Johnny Velasquez's agent. Agents assist in negotiating which mounts their jockeys ride on any day.

QUESTION # 75

While most of the 11 U.S. Triple Crown winners were favorites in the Belmont Stakes after winning the first two jewels of this feat, two were not? What were their names?

QUESTION # 76

What is the general rule of thumb regarding apprentice jockeys about weight allowances in any given race? Are there any weight allowances for female horses when they run?

ANSWER # 75

Neither Gallant Fox (1930) nor Assault (1948) was the favorite when they ran in the third jewel of the U.S. Triple Crown – the Belmont Stakes.

ANSWER # 76

Apprentice jockeys are allowed a 10 lb. weight allowance up until their fifth race, 7 lbs. up until their 35th race and 5 lbs. allowance for the 1st calendar year from the 35th race. The general rule of thumb is that there is nearly always a weight allowance for female horses.

QUESTION # 77

Did any foreign horse ever win the Kentucky Derby?

QUESTION # 78

Why is the use of Lasix, which prevents EPH (bleeding caused by the strain of exercise), so controversial today?

ANSWER # 77

The only time a foreign horse won the Kentucky Derby was Canonero II, the 1971 upset winner from Venezuela.

ANSWER # 78

Unknown in the 1960's, Lasix use today causes increased urinary output which can flush away traces of other illicit performance enhancing medications that would be otherwise present in the horse's bloodstream.

QUESTION # 79

Why should bettors pay attention to the letter and number "L1" in front of a horse that is entered in the race they are betting on?

QUESTION # 80

What two famous thoroughbreds shared the same nickname "Big Red?" One was a U.S. Triple Crown winner while his predecessor was able to win 21 out of the 22 races that he ran.

ANSWER # 79

L1 means that this horse has been given
Lasix for the first time which should increase
his chances of winning the race. Lasix
lessens fatigue, thereby giving the horse an
edge over other horses in the race.

ANSWER # 80

Both Secretariat - who won the U.S. Triple
Crown in 1973 – and Man o' War were
nicknamed "Big Red" because of their
chestnut color and stature. Secretariat's
Grand Sire, Nasrullah, is also the Grand
Grand Sire of 1977 Triple Crown winner,
Seattle Slew.

QUESTION # 81

Where are the backstretch and the
homestretch located on a racetrack?

QUESTION # 82

What outstanding percentages describe the
role of Afro-Americans in the early phase of
the Kentucky Derby?

ANSWER # 81

The backstretch is usually that long stretch directly across the track from the spectators where the stables are located (outside the rail). The homestretch is the area just before the finish line. The homestretch is an exciting area where horses feverishly attempt to find that last burst of energy and win.

ANSWER # 82

Thirteen of the fifteen riders in the first Kentucky Derby were Afro-Americans. Afro-American jockeys won 15 out of the first 28 races of the Kentucky Derby.

QUESTION # 83

When and where was the 1st racetrack built in the United States?

QUESTION # 84

What is Bookmaking and what organization was formed to give it legitimate, legal status in the U.S.?

ANSWER # 83

The 1st U.S. racetrack dates back to 1664 when Newmarket course was built on Salisbury Plains in Hempstead, Long Island, New York. The American Stud Book was organized in 1868. By 1890, 314 tracks were operating while 1894 saw the formation of the American Jockey Club.

ANSWER # 84

Bookmaking is the process of taking bets, calculating odds and paying out winners. Although Bookmaking is illegal, governing bodies have sanctioned other types of betting. At present, Off Track Betting (OTB) exists on Long Island in New York State. It is run by the State of New York.

QUESTION # 85

Who was the youngest jockey to win the
Triple Crown?

QUESTION # 86

What is a Handicap race?

ANSWER # 85

The youngest jockey to win the U.S. Triple Crown is retired jockey Steve Cauthen aboard Affirmed in 1978. In 1977, his earnings passed the 6 million mark he had set earlier. He was then called "The Six Million Dollar Man" and "Stevie Wonder." He later rode in England because of problems with weight.

ANSWER # 86

In a Handicap race, the runners have been "handicapped" by carrying more weight according to their performances in other races. The general idea is that all horses have an equal chance of being competitive in a race that is correctly handicapped.

QUESTION # 87

What is a Maiden race?

QUESTION # 88

What is a Allowance race?

ANSWER # 87

In a Maiden race, the key factor is that the runners have never won a race. Horses that may come from many different age groups carry the same weights and run without any "penalties." Two year olds run against two year olds and three year olds run against three year olds.

ANSWER # 88

In an allowance race, the runners run for a higher purse than that of a maiden race. These races are for horses that have broken its maiden, but are not ready for stakes races. It is a race other than claiming for which the racing secretary drafts certain conditions to determine weights.

QUESTION # 89

What is a Claiming race?

QUESTION # 90

Which thoroughbred racing horse legend still holds the speed record for two parts of the U.S. Triple Crown?

ANSWER # 89

In a claiming race, horses are all for sale for more or less the same price – the claiming price. In order to even up the odds, a better-than-class entry risks being lost at the claiming price. The strategy behind claiming a horse is that the interested party believes that it has a higher potential with training.

ANSWER # 90

Present-day record holder, Secretariat, ran the Kentucky Derby at 1:52 and the Belmont Stakes at 2:24 flat. After 25 years from the preceding winner (Citation in 1948), Secretariat crossed the finish line with a 31 length lead which was still six lengths more than Count Fleet's winning length in 1943.

QUESTION # 91

How many horses have brought perfect records to the Kentucky Derby and left the Derby undefeated? How many Derby winners were born in Kentucky?

QUESTION # 92

What is an Optional Claiming race?

ANSWER # 91

While eighteen horses entered the Derby undefeated, only five walked away with the same bragging rights: Regret (1915), Morvich (1922), Majestic Prince (1969), Seattle Slew (1977) and Smarty Jones (2004). Ninety seven winners were born in the Bluegrass State.

ANSWER # 92

An optional claiming race is a hybrid of an allowance and claiming race. It is initiated to increase the field (number of entries) size. If a horse does not fit the conditions, it can still run the race for the "tag" (up for sale).

QUESTION # 93

What is the difference between an entry and the field?

QUESTION # 94

What are the meanings of the following racetrack terms: Declared, Dead Heat, Disqualification and Distaff Race?

ANSWER # 93

An entry consists of two or more horses owned by the same stable or trained by the same trainer while running as a single betting unit (coupled). The bettor bets the Entry – if either horse wins, the bettor wins.

ANSWER # 94

"Declared" means that a stakes race horse is withdrawn prior to scratch time. A dead heat means a finish line tie of horses at the finish wire. Disqualification (DQ) means that the officials have changed the order of finish because of an infraction. A Distaff Race (female race) has fillies or mares or both.

QUESTION # 95

What special relationship exists between the two thoroughbreds named Alydar and Affirmed with regard to the U.S. Triple Crown?

QUESTION # 96

There are approximately 150 racetracks within the U.S. Where are following race tracks located: Pompano Park, Arlington Park, Gulfstream Park, Del Mar Racetrack, Calder Race Course, Suffolk Downs, Woodbine Racetrack, and Finger Lakes?

ANSWER # 95

When Affirmed was the last thoroughbred to win the U.S. Triple Crown in 1978, Alydar ran second to him in all three events. This had never happened in a Triple Crown before. One can only surmise that if Affirmed had never run, Alydar would have captured the title and entered the records.

ANSWER # 96

Locations are: Pompano Park (FL), Arlington Park (Chicago, IL), Gulfstream Park (Hallandale, FL), Del Mar Racetrack (CA), Calder Race Course (Miami), Suffolk Downs (East Boston), Woodbine Racetrack (near Toronto, Canada), and the Finger Lakes Racetrack (Farmington, NY, near Rochester).

QUESTION # 97

Which jockey won the Eclipse Award for Outstanding Jockey four times, was the United States leading jockey for seven times and holds the record of most career wins (9530) over Bill Shoemaker (8833)?

QUESTION # 98

What are the meanings of the following racetrack terms: Near Side, Withers, Hand, Length and Neck?

ANSWER # 97

As of April 2003, Panamanian jockey Laffit Alejandro Pincay, Jr. remains horse racing's winningest jockey. He won the Santa Anita Derby in 1668, 1972, 1973, 1976, 1978, 1982 and 1985 at Santa Anita Racetrack is located in Arcadia, California where he is spends his retirement.

ANSWER # 98

Near Side - left side of the horse (where to mount). "Withers" is the high point of a horse's shoulder. A hand is a measurement of the length from the withers to the ground (4 inches). Length is a measurement from the horse's head to its tail – 8'. Neck is the length of a horse's neck – ¼ of a length.

QUESTION # 99

What are the meanings of the following racetrack terms: Hotwalker, Lead Pad, Lock, Mudder and Mudlark?

QUESTION # 100

Did jockey, Willie Shoemaker, ever win the U.S. Triple Crown?

ANSWER # 99

A Hotwalker is the person who walks the horse after a race or exercise. A lead pad is the weight that is added if the jockey's weight doesn't meet the weight requirement. A lock is the term for a sure thing (winner). Mudders are horses that run well on muddy tracks. A mudlark is a superior mudder.

ANSWER # 100

While Willie Shoemaker won 8,833 races which included 4 Kentucky Derbies, 2 Preakness Stakes and 5 Belmont Stakes, the U.S. Triple Crown had always eluded him. He was the first jockey to ever amass over 100 million in winnings.

QUESTION # 101

What are the meanings of the following racetrack terms: Off Side, Overland, Overlay and Pari-mutual?

QUESTION # 102

Was there ever an Afro-American jockey who won the Triple Crown as we know it today?

ANSWER # 101

Off Side – horse's right side. Overland is
when horse is racing wide throughout race.
Overlay - horse has higher price than worth
(past performance). Pari-mutual (Fr.) -
wagering in which all money bet is divided up
among those who won, after taxes, takeout,
and other deductions have been made.

ANSWER # 102

Prior to the Triple Crown, an Afro-American
jockey, Willie Simms, won two Kentucky
Derbies aboard Ben Brush (1896) and Plaudit
(1898). One of these wins was followed by
wins aboard horses in both the Preakness
Stakes and Belmont Stakes, making him an
honorary winner of the Triple Crown.

QUESTION # 103

What are the meanings of the following racetrack terms: Pill, Pinhooker or Pinhook and Pocket?

QUESTION # 104

What are the meanings of the following racetrack terms: Pole, Post Parade and Prop?

ANSWER # 103

Pill – small numbered ball drawn to decide post position or who will claim a horse if more than one claimant; Pinhooker or Pinhook – one who buys at Auction to sell later (like flipping houses); and Pocket – where a rider is when a rider is boxed in both in front and alongside during a race.

ANSWER # 104

Pole – spaced markers that measure distances around track (quarter pole tells rider he is a quarter of a mile from the finish, not the start); Post Parade – horses move in front of stands going from paddock to post (start gate); and Prop – horse balks at start gate, stands flat-footed or brakes fast at fast run.

QUESTION # 105

How many owners and trainers have been responsible for winning more than one U.S. Triple Crown?

QUESTION # 106

What is a thoroughbred racehorse normally fed?

ANSWER # 105

Two owners and their respective trainers that year won twice. Belair Stud Stable and their trainer, James "Sunny Jim" Fitzsimmons, won with Gallant Fox in 1930 and Omaha in 1935. Calumet Farms and their trainer, Ben A. Jones, won with Whirlaway in 1941 and Citation in 1948.

ANSWER # 106

Aside from water, thoroughbred racehorses are fed hay, oats and Sweetfeed [molasses in candy form which might causes diarrhea if too much is easten] and Timothy [hay that cuts down on sweetness]. They are also fed the normal fare of grass carrots, apples, etc.

QUESTION # 107

What are the meanings of the following racetrack terms: Quarter Horse, Saddle Cloth, Shank and Sloppy?

QUESTION # 108

What are the meanings of the following racetrack terms: Shadow Roll, Simulcast, and Silks?

ANSWER # 107

Quarter horse – breed of horse especially fast for the quarter mile race; Saddle Cloth – cloth under saddle with post position # (maybe name); Shank – rope or strap attached to halter or bridle by which horse is led around; and Sloppy – condition where track is wet with firm bottom.

ANSWER # 108

Shadow Roll - lamb's wool which prevents horse from seeing their own shadow and jumping over it; Simulcast – televising races to other tracks, OTB, and other outlets for wagering purposes; Silks – cap and jacket worn by rider that designates owner of the horse.

QUESTION # 109

What is a Match Race and how does it function within the IMRA?

QUESTION # 110

While numerous, notarized match races have occurred over time, only four have involved Triple Crown winners. Which thoroughbreds have been matched and did any of the four Triple Crown winners emerge victorious? (Remember, many match races are challenges outside scheduled attended events).

ANSWER # 109

A Match Race is a race between two competitors, going head-to-head. It arose in horse racing when two entrants wanted to compete for bragging rights outside any scheduled event. The International Match Racing Association was created in 2009 to allow a sanctioned event.

ANSWER # 110

The four match races involving U.S. Triple Crown winners were: Man o' War versus Sir Barton (1920); Seabiscuit versus War Admiral (1938); Whirlaway versus Alsab (1942); and Assault versus Armed (1947). All four U.S. Triple Crown winners were defeated – Assault was beaten by 8 lengths.

QUESTION # 111

What are the meanings of the following racetrack terms: Spit the Bit; Valet and Yearling?

QUESTION # 112

How many winners of the Kentucky Derby held the post positions between 1 and 5? How many held the post position of 15?

ANSWER # 111

Spit the bit – fatigue sets in during a race and the horse stops running against the bit; Valet – the person who attends riders by keeping their wardrobe and equipment in order; and Yearling – a thoroughbred between the 1st New Years Day after being foaled and the next January 1st.

ANSWER # 112

The post position #2 had 29 while post position #1 had only 12 winners. Post position #3 had none while post positions #4 and #5 had 10 winners. Post position #15 had no winners.

QUESTION # 113

How did the filly, Ruffian - who was never beheaded in a race (never lost a head-to-head encounter with a competing horse or filly where she was overtaken – finally react when she was overtaken by Foolish Pleasure in a match race?

QUESTION # 114

What became of Ruffian after she tumbled over during her match race with Foolish Pleasure?

ANSWER # 113

Ruffian – who was never beheaded or beaten out in a regular race – was beheaded by her opponent in a match race where she was pitted against Foolish Pleasure. Unable to deal with the other horse's getting in front of her, Ruffian faltered in her step and fell over.

ANSWER # 114

Upon falling over, after losing the lead to Foolish Pleasure, Ruffian was put in a stable harness for rehabilitative reasons. Her excessive rejection of the harness caused such harm as to warrant humanely euthanizing her. This beloved filly is buried somewhere on Belmont Race Track.

QUESTION # 115

Who was the jockey who rode the legendary Secretariat to his record holding two jewels of the U.S. Triple Crown and actually won the Triple Crown? Was it Willie Shoemaker, Ron Turcotte or Eddie Arcaro?

QUESTION # 116

What are the meanings of the following racetrack terms: Tout, Also-Ran, Bear Out Book and Break?

ANSWER # 115

The jockey who won the U.S. Triple Crown
aboard Secretariat while breaking two records
(the Kentucky Derby & the Belmont Stakes)
that still stand today was Ron Turcotte in
1973. The trainer of Secretariat was Lucien
Laurin and the owner was Helen Bates
"Penny" Chenery Tweedy of Meadow Stable.

ANSWER # 116

A tout - racetrack deadbeat that suggests a
winner while looking for a reward; Also-Ran
means ran out of the money; Bear Out – to
drift or veer out to the outside of the track;
Book – jockey's record of riding "trips" or
rides; and Break – start of a race; train a horse
to accept saddle, bridle and rider.

QUESTION # 117

Which owners and trainers won the most
races at the Kentucky Derby?

QUESTION # 118

Which jockeys won the most races at the
Kentucky Derby and had the most mounts?

ANSWER # 117

The trainers who led the list of winners at the Kentucky Derby are Ben A. Jones who is #1 with 6 wins and H.J. Thompson is position #2 with 4 wins. They are followed by James "Sunny Jim" Fitzsimmons, Max Hirsch and D. Wayne Lucas each with 3 wins. Calumet Farms is the leading owner with 8 wins.

ANSWER # 118

Both Eddie Arcaro [who rode 2 Triple Crowns winners – Whirlaway (1941) and Citation (1948)] and Bill Hartack had the most wins at 5. Willie "The Shoe" Shoemaker followed with 4 wins. Shoemaker leads Arcaro with 26 mounts while Arcaro rode only 21 mounts – with more wins.

QUESTION # 119

What are the meanings of the following racetrack terms: Break Maiden, Card, Chute Close and Closer?

QUESTION # 120

Who is the oldest jockey to run the Kentucky Derby?

ANSWER # 119

Break Maiden – when a horse gets its 1st win;
Card – a day's racing program; Chute – an
extension of the stretch allowing a long,
straight run from the gate to the first turn;
Close – means gaining ground on the leader;
and Closer – means that this horse is capable
of catching up at the end of the race.

ANSWER # 120

The oldest jockey to ride in the Kentucky
Derby was Willie Shoemaker at 54 years of
age. He won the Derby aboard Ferdinand
and beat Alysheba the next year aboard this
thoroughbred in the Breeder's Cup Classic.
Even though he won 11 jewels of the U.S.
Triple Crown, he never won the Crown itself.

QUESTION # 121

What are the meanings of the following racetrack terms: Clubhouse turn, Cuppy, Dam, Sire, and Dwelt?

QUESTION # 122

Which jockey has an award created in his honor (2004) and named after him because he won a premier race of western U.S. nine times in his extraordinary career?

ANSWER # 121

Clubhouse turn – usually the turn on the right hand side of the track as seen from the stands; Cuppy – dirt track surface which is loose and dry; Dam – mother of the horse; Sire – father of the horse; Dwelt – horse breaks very slowly from the starting gate.

ANSWER # 122

Panamanian born Laffit Pincay, Jr. has the Laffit Pincay, Jr. Award named after him for his nine wins at the running of the Hollywood Gold Cup. This premier race of the western U.S. is run annually at Hollywood Park Race Track on a synthetic dirt track with a handicap format.

What distinction do the following three horses have in common: Regret, Genuine Risk and Winning Colors?

QUESTION # 124

What are the meanings of the following racetrack terms: Equine, Farrier, Fast Track Good Track and Heavy Track?

ANSWER #123

These three fillies have the distinction of being the only three fillies to ever win the Kentucky Derby in its 136 outings. Regret was the first to win in 1915. Sixty five years later in 1980, Genuine Risk won it. Finally in 1988, the Derby was won by Winning Colors.

ANSWER # 124

Equine – a horse; Farrier – blacksmith, who makes and attaches horseshoes; Fast Track – condition of dirt track where faster than normal times are recorded; Good Track – dry track surface between sloppy and fast; and Heavy Track – a running surface drier than muddy and very slow.

QUESTION # 125

Besides the traditional draping of the blanket of Black-Eyed Susans across the shoulders of the winning horse, what other honors are bestowed on the owner(s)?

QUESTION # 126

What are the meanings of the following racetrack terms: Juvenile, Lugging In, One-Run Type, On the nose, Outrider?

ANSWER # 125

The jockey's colors are painted on the Pimlico weathervane until the next Preakness Stakes. The owner(s) receive a half-size sterling replica trophy of the Woodlawn Vase Trophy valued at 1 million dollars easily in 1983. The original vase was designed by Tiffany & Company in 1860.

ANSWER # 126

Juvenile – two year old; Lugging In – horse which tends to lag toward the back of the pack during the early stages of race before monunting a late run; On the nose – a bet to win; and Outrider – official who rides a pony and leads the thoroughbreds onto the track from the Paddock area.

QUESTION # 127

What are the names of the one gelding and three fillies that hold the distinction of winning the Belmont Stakes?

QUESTION # 128

Who owned the two horses Armed and U.S. Triple Crown winner, Assault when Armed beat Assault in a match race by 8 lengths?

ANSWER # 127

The gelding's name is Crème Fraiche (1985) while the names of the three fillies are Ruthless (1867), Rags to Riches (1905) and Tanya (2007).

ANSWER # 128

Assault was owned by King Ranch in Texas while the winner of the match race, Armed, was owned by Calumet Farm in Lexington, in Kentucky.

QUESTION # 129

What are the ingredients in the traditional drink of the Kentucky Derby, the Mint Julep?

QUESTION # 130

What steps are taken in the preparation of a Mint Julep?

ANSWER # 129

Mint Julep ingredients: 4 fresh mint sprigs, 2 and ½ oz. of bourbon whiskey, 1 tsp. of powdered sugar, and 2 tsp. of tap water.

ANSWER # 130

Mint Julep preparation: muddle mint leaves, powdered sugar, and water in a Collins glass. Fill the glass with shaved or crushed ice and add boubon. Top with more ice and garnish with a mint sprig.

QUESTION # 131

What are the meanings of the following racetrack terms: Post, Rabbit, Route, Salute and Shed Area?

QUESTION # 132

What is the name of the only U.S. Triple Crown winner who sired another U.S. Triple Crown winner?

ANSWER # 131

Post – the starting gate or time a race will begin; Rabbit – special horse entered to insure a fast pace (possibly to fatigue competition); Route – a long race, a mile or more; Salute – wave of whip by jockey to stewards after a race in customery request to dismount.

ANSWER # 132

The only U.S. Triple Crown winner to sire another U.S. Triple Crown winner was Gallant Fox (1930) who sired Omaha (1935).

QUESTION # 133

Has every Belmont Stakes race been run at Belmont Park?

QUESTION # 134

What are the meanings of the following racetrack terms: Shoe Board, Shut Out, and Sloppy Track?

ANSWER # 133

No, the first Belmont Stakes was run at
Jerome Park.

ANSWER # 134

Shoe board – a sign listing the kinds of shoes
to be worn by each entrant; Shut Out –
failing to get a bet in before the race begins
(usually from spending too much time
watching the odds board); Sloppy Track – a
running surface in which water stands on the
surface prior to sinking in or running off.

QUESTION # 135

What are the ingredients in the traditional drink of the Preakness Stakes, the Black-Eyed Susan?

QUESTION # 136

What steps are taken in the preparation of a Black-Eyed Susan?

ANSWER # 135

Black-Eyed Susan ingredients: 1 and ¼ cup of vodka, 4 cups of orange juice, 1 and ¼ cup of light rum, ice ring, ¾ cup of triple sec, 1 tbsp. fresh lime juice, and 4 cups of pineapple juice.

ANSWER # 136

Black-Eyed Susan preparation: chill all ingredients. Just before serving – combine in a punch bowl. Unfold ice ring and float in punch bowl. Serve in large glasses. This recipe makes 10 large servings.

QUESTION # 137

Which horse race has the largest attendance in the U.S. and which horse runs 2nd?

QUESTION # 138

Which U.S. Triple Crown winner was owned by the wife of Hertz-Rent-A-Car and rode by Hall of Fame inductee, Johnny Longdon.

ANSWER # 137

Because it is the first jewel in the U.S. Triple Crown, the Kentucky Derby has the largest attendance while the Preakness Stakes has the 2nd largest attendance.

ANSWER # 138

U.S. Triple Crown winner, Count Fleet (1943) was owned by Mrs. John D. Hertz who did not think very highly of the colt at first.

QUESTION # 139

What are the ingredients in the traditional drink of the Belmont Stakes, the Belmont Breeze since 1999? (Hint: It is not an ice cold can of Budweiser).

QUESTION # 140

What steps are taken in the preparation of a Belmont Breeze?

ANSWER # 139

Belmont Breeze ingredients: 1 and ½ oz. of bourbon, ½ oz. Dry Sack Medium Dry Sherry, ½ oz. fresh lemon juice, ½ oz. simple syrup, 1 and ½ oz. fresh orange juice, splash of cranberry juice, 5 mint leaves, 1 mint sprig, and 1 orange zest.

ANSWER # 140

Belmont Breeze preparation: shake all ingredients with ice. Strain into a chilled cocktail glass. Garnish with fresh mint sprig and orange peel.

QUESTION # 141

What makes up the Tack (all the equipment that goes on a horse along with the jockey)?

QUESTION # 142

What are the names of the three foundation sires that all registered thoroughbreds can be traced back to with regard to heritage?

ANSWER # 141

Horse equipment includes the following: saddle cloth, saddle, bit (in mouth - metal, etc.), blinders [prevent peripheral distractions], halter, stirrups, bridle, reins, and horseshoes [bar shoes for injury protection, calk for shoes on wet surfaces].

ANSWER # 142

The three foundation sires (Arabian, Barb, or Turkish) are as follows: The Darley Arabian, The Godolphin Arabian (or Godolphin Barb) and The Byerley Turk had been brought to England from Yemen in the late 17th and early 18th centuries and crossed with English and imported mares.

QUESTION # 143

Which thoroughbred is considered to be the most successful sire in the history of U.S. thoroughbred racing history?

QUESTION # 144

What are the meanings of the following racetrack terms: Layoff, sophomore, Stud and Tack?

ANSWER # 143

Northern Dancer holds this distinction. It sired 10 stakes winners out of its first 21 "firstlings." Two of these, War Admiral and Man o' War – went on to be U.S. Triple Crown winners.

ANSWER # 144

Layoff – a rest varying in length from two months to two years; sophomore is a three-year-old (a sophomore because horses do not race until their second year); stud – a breeding stallion; and Tack – all of the equipment that goes on the horse along with the jockey.

QUESTION # 145

Is there a trophy offered to the owner(s) of the winning horse at the end of the Belmont Stakes like the replica of the Woodlawn Vase that is offered to the owner(s) of the Preakness Stakes?

QUESTION # 146

What are the meanings of the following racetrack terms: Take up, Tongue Strap or Tie, and Baby Race?

ANSWER # 145

The owner(s) is awarded the August Belmont Memorial Cup which is a solid silver bowl and cover made by Tiffany and Co. It is 18 inches tall and 15 inches across and 14 inches at the base. Atop the cover is a silver figure of 1869 Belmont winner Fenian. Owner(s) hold it for one year.

ANSWER # 146

Take up – to pull a horse up sharply during the running in order to prevent contact with another horse; Tongue Strap or Tie – cloth or leather band used to tie down a horse's tongue s to prevent the tongue from interfering with breathing; Baby Races are dashes for two-year-olds.

QUESTION # 147

Which winner of the U.S. Triple Crown winner has the distinction of being the only Triple Crown winner to beat another Triple Crown winner? Who beat who in the race?

QUESTION # 148

In what year did the Belmont Stakes become an annual purse of $1 million dollars?

ANSWER # 147

Seattle Slew has the distinction of beating another Triple Crown winner in a separate race. Seattle Slew eventually raced and beat Affirmed – it was not a match race.

ANSWER # 148

The year that the Belmont Stakes was put at $1 million dollars annually was 1998.

QUESTION # 149

Which U.S. Triple Crown winner was
nicknamed "Mr. Longtail"?

QUESTION # 150

Is there a trophy offered to the owner(s) of
the winning horse at the end of the Kentucky
Derby like the replica of the Woodlawn Vase
that is offered to the owner(s) of the
Preakness Stakes and the August Belmont
Trophy Cup that is offered to the winner of
the Belmont Stakes?

ANSWER # 149

Whirlaway was nicknamed "Mr. Longtail."
This 1941 U.S. Triple Crown winner was a
crowd pleaser thrilling spectators with his
spectacular last-to-first bursts that became his
trademark. This short, flaming chestnut
would make these bursts with his tail
streaming like a pennant.

ANSWER # 150

The Kentucky Derby winner is awarded a
solid gold handcrafted trophy (excluding the
horse and rider which are cast in a mold).
The trophy is topped by a 18-karat gold horse
and rider and includes horseshoe shaped
handles. It is 22 inches tall and weighs 56
ounces, excluding its jade base.

Made in United States
Troutdale, OR
05/01/2024